Cyber-Savvy Parenting
Protecting Your Children Online

Table of Contents

Chapter 1. Introduction

In this increasingly digitized world, ensuring the safety of our children online becomes a paramount responsibility. Even if you feel lost in the tech jargon and feel like you're navigating uncharted territories, worry not! Our Special Report on "Cyber-Savvy Parenting: Protecting Your Children Online" has got you covered. Crafted with simplicity and ease of understanding in mind, it unravels the complexities of the digital world and equips you with the critical knowledge you need to create a safe online experience for your children. Encapsulating crucial subjects such as internet privacy, appropriate content curation, and effective ways to combat cyberbullying, our report promises a comprehensive guide for every parent. You don't need to be a techie to protect your children online; you need the right strategies - and that's precisely what this special report is offering. So, let's join hands and make the internet a safer place for our youngsters. Get your copy today and take the first step to become a cyber-savvy parent!

Chapter 2. Understanding the Digital Landscape: A Primer for Parents

Understanding the digital landscape is integral to knowing how best to protect your children online. Picture it as a vast city - with its shiny towers and dark alleys, busy streets and deserted corners. Interpreting this digital city and teaching your children to navigate it safely is a key step to cyber-safe parenting.

2.1. Demystifying the Internet

The internet, simply put, is a global network of computers. When your child uses a laptop, phone, or tablet to hop online, they are joining this massive network. Activities range from checking their emails and posting on social media to playing online games, downloading music, and doing homework.

Internet usage generates a plethora of data - often sensitive and private - such as login credentials, emails, files, photos, and more. This data is stored in various locations such as the device itself, external hard drives, or in 'the cloud'— a term that refers to servers accessed over the internet. Consequently, managing these data becomes essential to ensure your child's safety online.

2.2. Social Media: Pros and Cons

Social media is a significant component of the digital landscape. It's where your child connects with friends, creates and shares content, and partakes in online communities. Platforms such as Facebook, Instagram, TikTok, Snapchat, and others are incredibly popular among young users.

While social media can foster creativity and social skills, it can also be a source of inappropriate content, cyberbullying, and privacy concerns. Striking a balance between its advantages and drawbacks requires diligent parental guidance.

2.3. Online Gaming World

Online video games are more than just recreational activities. Many modern games have inbuilt communication systems, allowing players to chat and interact with others worldwide. While this interaction can promote teamwork and strategic thinking, it can also expose young gamers to potential online predators or cyberbullies.

Games often include in-app purchases, which might lead to overspending if not checked. Understanding how these games work, their rating, and their in-game features is crucial in curating a safe gaming environment for your children.

2.4. The Prism of Privacy

In today's internet era, privacy is continually evolving. Information that your child shares online, willingly or unknowingly, may be used against them or to exploit them. Privacy concerns also include 'cookies,' which are small pieces of data stored in your web browser by websites to track online behavior.

Equipping yourself with information about these privacy issues is essential. It helps you to create informed rules about your child's internet usage and enables you to share practical tips for them to protect their online presence.

2.5. Content Consumption and Exposure

The internet is an ocean of content – it's up to the user to sail towards enlightening educational videos, engaging user blogs, or submerge into mature or inappropriate content. Explicit or incorrect information exposure can influence a child's psyche, making it vital to set up proper parental controls or use kid-friendly search engines.

2.6. Cyberbullying: A Modern Threat

Modern technology has unfortunately given birth to a 21st-century problem that redefines bullying - cyberbullying. It refers to any form of bullying that occurs online, either through social networks, instant messaging, or email. Understanding the signs of cyberbullying, learning how to report it, and talking about it openly with your children are key to address this challenge.

2.7. Navigating the Digital Landscape Safely: A Summary

In conclusion, understanding the digital landscape is vital for safe navigation. Learning about the internet's complexities aids you in having informed discussions with your children regarding their online activities. Understanding their favorite social media platforms, how their chosen games work, the importance of online privacy, the type of content they might encounter, and the prevalent threat of cyberbullying are all crucial areas to explore.

In succeeding chapters, we'll delve deeper into these topics. We will equip you with strategies to guide your children through these digital alleys and avenues safely. Together, we'll ensure our young ones can reap the tremendous benefits of the internet without getting lost in its labyrinth. So, strengthen your resolve as we embark on this journey of cyber-savvy parenting.

Chapter 3. Cyber Threats to Children: A Comprehensive Overview

The digital world can be as dangerous as it is educational and entertaining, especially for children. It's imperative that parents are well-informed about the cyber threats their kids could potentially face.

3.1. Understanding Cyber Threats

Internet threats to children are as varied as they are numerous, with new threats emerging as rapidly as technology evolves. They range from malicious software, known as malware, and harmful content, to scams and cyber predators.

Malware, which includes viruses, spyware, and ransomware, can infect a child's device and allow a third party to control it, frequently with the aim of stealing sensitive information. Harmful content encompasses sites and online posts that are sexually explicit, violent, or encourage dangerous behavior, substance abuse, or self-harm. Scams often take the form of clickbait, presenting enticing links or messages designed to make the user reveal personal data. Cyber predators manipulate children to gain personal information or exploit them sexually, often posing as a child themselves.

3.2. Risks of Social Media and Online Games

When it comes to social media and online gaming platforms, it's crucial to realize they provide an environment conducive to cyber threats. Cyberbullying can occur, involving abusive messages or the sharing of personal images without consent. Sexual predators may also employ these platforms, posing a significant risk to children who may innocently engage in online chat or participate in multiplayer games.

Additionally, there are risks associated with oversharing. Many children aren't aware of the perils of revealing too much personal information on social media, including their location, school, and other identifying details. This information can be used by malevolent individuals for nefarious purposes such as stalking, doxing, or identity theft.

3.3. Critical Issues of Privacy

Children's privacy online is a significant concern. Without proper knowledge and controls, children might inadvertently share sensitive personal data, such as their full name, address, or photographs, that could be misused by cybercriminals. Furthermore, they can become targets of phishing campaigns, wherein attackers trick them into supplying crucial information, like login credentials and credit card details.

Another concern is online tracking. Websites and applications use various technologies, such as cookies and device identifiers, to track users across the web, creating detailed profiles of their online activities. These profiles can be used to serve targeted ads or can be sold to third parties, with serious implications for privacy.

3.4. Harmful Content and Inappropriate Material

The internet hosts a vast amount of content, not all of which is suitable for children. Some of it can be harmful, such as exposure to graphic violence, explicit adult content, hate speech, cyberbullying, and content promoting dangerous behaviors like substance abuse or self-harm.

Moreover, children might come across websites or chat rooms that promote harmful ideologies like discrimination, violence, and self-harm. These can significantly influence a child's thinking and behavior, having lasting impacts on their mental and emotional well-being.

3.5. Cyberbullying: A Digital Epidemic

Cyberbullying is a rapidly growing issue facing today's youth that involves the use of digital technology to harass, embarrass, or threaten others. Because it can happen anywhere, anytime, the victim may feel like there's no escape.

The impact of cyberbullying is significant. It can lead to severe mental health issues, including anxiety, depression, and even suicidal thoughts. It's vital to educate children about safe online communication to prevent cyberbullying and to encourage them to speak up if they become victims.

3.6. Strategies to Keep Children Safe Online

We've understood the risks; now, let's turn our focus on strategies to safeguard our children from these internet threats. It starts with educating your child about the potential risks and explaining the importance of keeping their personal information private.

Implement parental controls and filters on your children's devices to restrict access to unsuitable content. Moreover, setting device usage times could limit their exposure to potential online threats.

Ensure to maintain an open line of communication with your children, encouraging them to communicate any uncomfortable online experiences. Regularly check their devices and browse through installed apps or browsing history to spot any signs of having been at risk.

Remember, while the digital space can encompass numerous threats, it also brings opportunities for learning and development. As a parent, remaining vigilant, informed, and engaged can go a long way in ensuring your children harness the internet's benefits while staying shielded from the dangers lurking within it.

Chapter 4. Encouraging Online Safety: Simple Steps to Follow

Online safety is a broad subject, although it may initially appear to be quite straightforward. It covers everything from secure passwords to privacy settings and how to behave courteously on social media. As parents, it's our job to provide guidance and advice, along with a little direct supervision, to ensure that our children are navigating the internet safely.

4.1. Setting Up a Safe Online Environment

Start by creating a safe online environment as the foundation of your child's internet experience. Look for devices with built-in safety features, and use content filters on search engines, YouTube, and even on your home network. Be aware that no tool is 100% foolproof, but they can help to filter out the majority of inappropriate content.

Installation of an antivirus software is a must. It will protect your device from potential harmful attacks which might put your privacy and data at risk. Always ensure that the software is up to date for optimum protection.

Another significant aspect is to set up their email accounts until they're genuinely mature enough to do it themselves. Teach them the importance of a strong password and do not make it a habit of saving their passwords, as this might leave their account vulnerable.

Ad blockers can prevent annoying and potentially malicious ads. They're not perfect, but they can significantly improve your child's online experience while reducing risks.

4.2. The Importance of Privacy Settings

Understand the privacy settings on all the platforms and applications your children are using. Most social media platforms have an option to set their account to private, which means only people they've approved can see their posts.

Show them how to turn off location services for certain apps, ensuring not every post they make tags their location. Talk about the importance of not sharing private information, like their home address, school name or telephone number online.

Furthermore, teach them to be wary of friend requests from people they don't know, and to never meet with anyone they only know online without a trusted adult present.

4.3. Dealing with Social Media

Social media can be complicated and intimidating, but it's a major part of most children's online experiences. Create your accounts and have your kids friend or follow you. Also, know their friends if possible. The internet, especially social media, shouldn't be an unknown world to parents.

Promote internet kindness and empathy. Teach them about the impact of their words and actions over the internet. Ensure they know it's just as essential to be nice online as it is offline.

Cyberbullying is a severe issue on social media platforms. Make sure your child feels comfortable enough to talk to you if they're being bullied. If your child reports this behavior to you, take it seriously.

4.4. Understanding Screen Time and Setting Boundaries

The time a child spends online is just as important as what they're doing during that time. Outline clear rules about internet and tech usage. These can be specific as you like, but they should definitely include restrictions on sharing personal information and posting photos.

Limit the screen time for young kids. Most devices offer parental controls that allow you to limit how long, and at what times, your children can use their devices.

Additionally, it is advisable to make sure your child's device usage isn't interfering with sleep, school, or time spent outside or reading.

4.5. Having Open Conversations

Possibly the most effective tool you have for helping your child stay safe online is dialogue. Regular open conversations can make a big difference. Discuss their favorite websites, what they're into right now, and the basics of internet safety.

Warn them about online scams such as click bait, pop-up warnings, and 'free' offers, which usually have a catch. This could be a good way to discuss the importance of skepticism when online.

Make sure your child knows that they can come to you if they're feeling uncomfortable or uneasy about something they've seen online.

Online safety might seem overwhelming, but take one step at a time. The internet is a huge part of our lives, and teaching young people about how to use it responsibly and safely is an important part of preparing them for the world.

Chapter 5. Defining Boundaries: Strategies for Internet Access and Screen Time

Establishing boundaries in the digital environment is pivotal to keep your children safe and healthy. It revolves around setting access limits, monitoring screen time, and navigating the intricate web of online content. This chapter will guide you through each of these aspects in detail, ensuring you not only understand the challenges but are capable of effectively addressing them.

5.1. Understanding the Importance of Boundaries

Internet access and times spent on screens can have a notable impact on your children's developmental, physical, and mental health. Unrestricted screen time can expose children to inappropriate content, disrupt their sleep patterns, cause physical discomfort, and even contribute to obesity. Setting boundaries, therefore, can be seen as a preventive measure, ensuring healthier habits and safer navigation in the digital space.

5.2. Creating Internet Access Boundaries

The first step in defining boundaries is determining what sites are appropriate for your child. You can achieve this through internet filters, age restrictions, and scrutinizing the content before your child is exposed to it. Parental controls can be set on most devices, allowing you to restrict access to certain websites and apps. Make sure to check the privacy settings and ensure personal data is not being collected or shared.

The establishment of rules regarding the types of sites and content that are deemed suitable also plays a crucial role. Combine these methods with continuous monitoring to ensure your children are following the guidelines appropriately.

5.3. Crafting a Screen Time Schedule

Establishing a screen time schedule helps regulate the amount of time your children spend on digital devices. This should take into account their age, hobbies, and daily routines. The American Academy of Pediatrics suggests no screen time for children below 18 months, one hour per day for children aged 2-5, and consistent limits for children aged 6 and above. However, remember that these are suggested guidelines. Consider your child's needs, personality, and interests when developing a schedule.

Develop the habit of "unplugged" family time. This could be during meals, just before bedtime, or even setting aside an entire day of the week to encourage interpersonal communication and engagement.

5.4. Encouraging Healthy Screen Time Habits

Beyond setting screen time limits, it is important to promote healthy habits while using digital devices. Encourage your children to take breaks every 20-30 minutes to prevent eye strain. Make sure they maintain a considerable distance from the device's screen.

Try to ensure that screen time does not interfere with physical activity. Encourage your children to get up, move around, and engage in physical activities like cycling, playing catch, or even a leisurely walk in the park.

5.5. Engaging in Open Dialogue

It's essential to keep the lines of communication open about their digital experiences. Talk to your children about why specific boundaries have been put in place and make the conversation a two-way street. Let their voices be heard, as this will make them more likely to adhere to the rules set.

5.6. Revisiting and Adjusting Boundaries

As your child grows, their digital needs may change. Revisit the boundaries periodically and make amendments accordingly. This also ensures that the safety measures remain robust and relevant as technological advancements introduce new challenges.

Building boundaries around internet usage and screen time is not about constraining your children but about creating a balance. It's about ensuring they reap the benefits of the digital world without compromising their overall well-being. Guidelines set respectfully and reasonably can foster a healthy, safe, and beneficial relationship with technology. It might feel difficult at times, but remember, you're not alone in this journey, and your efforts are contributing to the long-term welfare and success of your child.

Chapter 6. Internet Privacy: Teaching Kids to Safeguard Personal Information

In the digital age, the concept of privacy has taken on a whole new dimension. As children interact with the world through screens, it is important for them to understand that - like the tangible world - the cyber world also has its boundaries and how important it is for these to be respected and protected. Let's delve into the key aspects of Internet Privacy, teaching our kids how to safeguard their personal information online.

6.1. Understanding Internet Privacy

Before we jump into the specifics of teaching our children about internet privacy, it's vital that we ourselves have a thorough understanding. Every time we log onto the internet, we leave behind a 'digital footprint.' This trace, pattern, or trail of data can be tracked by others: think social media posts, websites visited, or even emails sent. The risk lies in the potential for misuse of this information, making safeguarding privacy critical.

It's significant to keep in mind that while the internet may feel anonymous due to the physical distance involved, it's anything but that. Data shared is data exposed - to individuals, companies, and other entities. Information protection becomes a valuable skill to learn, teach, and implement.

6.2. The Line Between Public and Private

Just as certain topics are considered 'private' in real-life conversations, there are certain types of information that are considered private online. Generally, these encompass personal identifiers such as one's real name, home address, phone numbers, social security numbers, school names/locations, password and credit card information. Sensitive health information should also be considered private.

Educating kids about the clear line distinguishing public and private information is essential. Digital citizenship encourages honoring this division much like one would respect the same in a real-world scenario.

6.3. Online Oversharing: A Common Pitfall

One of the prolific issues that contribute to breeches in internet privacy is the act of 'oversharing.' A casual tweet or a seemingly harmless Facebook post can give away more information than intended. Personal photos uploaded may contain meta-data that could reveal the precise location and time those pictures were taken.

Inculcating mindful posting habits is essential. Children should be encouraged to think twice before posting on the internet or sharing data. Model thoughtful sharing by discussing your own social media routines, emphasizing how you too have to be cautious with your posts.

6.4. Password Protection and Security Measures

Teaching children about creating strong, unique passwords and the importance of changing them regularly goes a long way to protect their online accounts. Discuss the risks of sharing passwords, even with close friends. A useful analogy could be to liken passwords to toothbrushes - not something you would want to share!

Ensure they're aware of the importance of log-out procedures especially on public computers, and the necessity of two-factor authentication - an extra layer of security. They should understand never to click on suspicious links, or download files from an unverified digital source, since these can lead to cyber threats such as hacking or malware.

6.5. Privacy Settings and Safe Browsing

Guide your child to schedule a regular check of privacy settings across all social media platforms, and browsers they use. Teach them to understand the fine print in 'Terms and Conditions' before accepting - this will promote mindful engagement with digital platforms.

Finally, emphasize the importance of safe browsing. Using secure, kid-friendly search engines and setting up parental controls can help protect children from inadvertent exposure to potentially harmful content.

6.6. Open Dialogues: Encouraging Communication

Children might encounter unexpected facets of the internet that make them uncomfortable or unsafe. Create an environment conducive for open conversations about such experiences. Kids should know that they can approach parents or caregivers without the fear of repercussions or judgment.

By teaching our children about safeguarding personal information on the internet, we not only protect them from potential threats, we also empower them to navigate the digital world with confidence and responsibility. Learning, adapting, and teaching internet privacy measures needs to be an ongoing process, a shared journey with our kids as both the online world and its challenges continually evolve.

Chapter 7. Decoding Cyberbullying: Signs, Impacts, and Preventive Measures

In the broad spectrum of the digital world, cyberbullying stands as a prevalent issue that threatens young children's mental and emotional health. This chapter seeks to provide a comprehensive understanding of cyberbullying, outlining the principal signs, the impacts it can have on children, and preventive strategies parents can adopt.

7.1. Unraveling Cyberbullying

Cyberbullying is the act of harassing, threatening, or intimidating someone over the internet. This form of bullying takes advantage of the anonymity and the broad reach that the internet provides to cause harm unlike conventional bullying. Cyberbullying incidents can range from spreading rumors, sending unsolicited messages, posting hurtful comments, and, in some severe cases, impersonating the victim online.

7.2. Recognizing the Signs of Cyberbullying

Identifying cyberbullying can be challenging, especially considering the covert nature of online activities. However, some notable signs can indicate if your child is a victim of cyberbullying:

1. An abrupt change in their online activity, either excessive use or

complete withdrawal from their favorite platforms could signal distress.

2. Unexplained emotional responses after using the internet, which could range from anger and frustration to isolation and depression.

3. The reluctance to discuss online activities or discussions.

4. Noticeable decline in academic performance can also be traced back to cyberbullying.

5. Frequent mood swings, sleep disturbances, or a sudden change in friend circles.

Being aware of these signs is the first step towards addressing and combating cyberbullying.

7.3. The Impact of Cyberbullying

The effects of cyberbullying on children can be traumatizing, potentially impacting their psychological, emotional and physical well-being.

7.3.1. Psychological Impact

Consistent harassment online can lead to significant stress and anxiety, symptoms often associated with Post Traumatic Stress Disorder (PTSD). It can also catalyze the onset of other mental health conditions such as depression and suicidal ideation.

7.3.2. Emotional Impact

Victims of cyberbullying can face serious emotional turmoil. They may experience a broad range of negative emotions such as anger, fear, confusion, and embarrassment. Often they feel trapped since the attacks continue outside the physical confines of school or neighborhood.

7.3.3. Physical Impact

The psychological and emotional stress of cyberbullying can manifest into physical symptoms. Victims may suffer from somatic complaints such as headaches, stomachaches, sleep problems, and even self-harm.

7.4. Preventive Measures against Cyberbullying

As a parent, there are numerous strategies you can adopt to protect your child from cyberbullying:

1. Regular Communication: Keep the lines of communication open with your child. Encourage them to share their online experiences and educate them about the potential dangers of the digital world.

2. Online Etiquette: Teach your child the basics of digital etiquette, including respect for others' beliefs and opinions. Remind them that the anonymity of the internet doesn't provide a license to harm others.

3. Privacy Measures: Set up privacy controls on your children's online platforms and remind them not to share sensitive personal information online.

4. Monitor Online Activity: Regularly review your child's online activities. Utilize parental control software and apps to limit access or filter out harmful content.

5. Report and Block: Teach your child to report any cyberbullying incidents to you, their school, or directly to the online platform. Ensure they know how to block or report the bully on the platform.

Remember, understanding cyberbullying, its signs, impacts, and preventions is the first step towards creating a safe digital environment for your child. Equipped with this knowledge, you can effectively navigate your child's journey through their digital life.

23

Chapter 8. Social Media and Children: Navigating the New Age Networking

Social media is omnipresent and largely unavoidable in today's tech-dependent society. It has significantly transformed the way we communicate, influencing every age group, including our children. As children navigate this new age of networking, it's essential to understand the potentials and pitfalls that come with it. This chapter provides an in-depth analysis of how children interact with social media and the internet and presents practical strategies parents can adopt to ensure a safe online experience for them.

8.1. Understanding the Landscape

The digital terrain consists of a myriad of social media platforms - Instagram, TikTok, Snapchat, YouTube, Facebook, WhatsApp, and many more. Each platform harbors distinctive features, different levels of privacy controls, and various content types, which can have diverse effects on children's online experience. Understanding these platforms, their distinctive features, and the potential risks associated with them is the first step towards protecting your children.

Instagram, for instance, is image-centric, known for its photos and short videos. Twitter enables the dissemination of thoughts in compact sentences, while TikTok is popular for its music-infused, engaging short videos. Facebook provides a holistic social experience with its news feed, allowing photos, videos, and text. Snapchat offers image messaging and has gained traction with the younger crowd due to its ephemeral feature - with messages, images, and videos disappearing after viewing.

Each platform carries different types of content, some of which may not be suitable for children. For instance, the open nature of Twitter can expose children to heated debates or sensitive topics. Instagram's focus on visually perfect representation may perpetuate unrealistic standards of beauty which can impact the self-esteem of youngsters. Understanding the uniqueness of each platform can aid in making informed decisions regarding which platforms are suitable for your children.

8.2. Assessing Online Privacy

Privacy is a cornerstone of online safety. Each social networking site has varying privacy settings, enabling users to control who can see their content and how they can interact with it. Yet children might not fully comprehend these settings or the consequences of neglecting them. Therefore, parents' role in overseeing and adjusting these settings is crucial.

For instance, on Facebook, users can adjust who can see their posts, who can send friend requests, and even who can look them up using the email or phone number linked to their account. Instagram allows users to make their accounts private, approving followers manually, and also offers options to filter or disable comments.

It's advisable for parents to review these settings periodically with their children and explain their importance. Guide them to set their accounts to private, only accept friend or follow requests from people they know, and to limit what personal information they share.

8.3. Encouraging Safe Sharing

While sharing moments from our daily lives has become second nature, it's vital to emphasize to children the potential risks of unfiltered sharing. Consider running through a checklist before posting: Would you be comfortable with everyone seeing this? Does it reveal too much information? Could it harm your future reputation?

Highlight that once shared online, information can be cached or copied and may remain online indefinitely. Discuss with your children the potential issues of sharing personal details, revealing locations, or posting inappropriate content. Encourage them to think before they post and secure their online reputation. It's like the well-known saying, "Think Before You Ink," but updated for the digital age.

8.4. Handling Online Interactions

Online platforms provide an arena for interactions with both known and unknown digital citizens. While this can broaden one's social horizons, it also exposes children to potential cyberbullying or online predators. Encourage open dialogue about their online experiences, highlight the importance of respectful discourse, and educate them on tactful ways to handle negative comments or unsolicited messages.

Make it clear that they should approach you for support if they ever have unsettling online experiences. Set up a system - they can come to you immediately with anything they find uncomfortable, and, if appropriate, report to the platform or even law enforcement.

8.5. Nurturing Digital Literacy

Digital literacy involves the ability to analyze information found online. As information sources broaden, disinformation, misinformation, and fake news proliferate. Use real-life examples to explain how not everything they see or read online is accurate or true.

Teach them to assess the credibility of information by cross-checking from multiple sources and to verify the sources before sharing it with others. It's also important that they understand the manipulative intent behind emotionally charged clickbait headlines.

Navigating social media safely may appear daunting, but with the right knowledge and strategies, it is achievable. As parents, we need not eliminate digital experiences but rather help our children manage them responsibly. In doing so, we can convert the digital terrain from a potential minefield into a platform for personal growth and learning. Education, involvement, and open conversations are our most potent tools against the potential perils of social media. Let's use them wisely to ensure our children have a healthy online experience. And remember, we're learning too. In guiding our children, we become cyber-savvy parents ourselves.

Chapter 9. Age-Appropriate Content: Guiding Your Child's Digital Consumption

As we venture into the ever-evolving world of the internet, the real challenge lies in helping our children consume online content that is suitable for their age, developmental stage, and values. Striking the right balance between guidance and granting freedom is key to fostering learning, growth, and digital literacy.

9.1. Understanding Age-Appropriate Content

Age-appropriate content refers to the media content designed and marked suitable for specific age groups based on the cognitive, social, and emotional stages of a child. This can involve blocking explicit material or limiting internet access time, depending on your child's age and maturity.

Children respond differently to online content, and what's appropriate for one child may not be suitable for another even in the same age group. Understanding your child's individual temperament, maturity level, and ability to process information is essential in determining what content is appropriate.

9.2. Establishing Clear Guidelines

Having clear guidelines and rules about internet use can help your child understand what is acceptable and what isn't. Build a culture of trust and communication, allowing them to approach you if they stumble upon confusing or inappropriate content.

Establish device-free zones and times in your household to ensure your child doesn't over-indulge in screen time. Promoting collaboration in setting up regulations promotes a sense of responsibility and understanding of why such rules exist. This approach is more likely to be effective than forcibly enforcing regulations upon them.

9.3. Leveraging the Power of Parental Controls

Parental controls are digital tools that help you limit your child's online activities. These tools can help you filter and block inappropriate content, limit screen time, monitor online activities, restrict app downloads, and even track your child's location for safety.

Most modern operating systems and devices come with in-built parental control options. Also, numerous specialized applications are available to offer more tailored controls. Be sure to conduct thorough research before choosing a solution, taking into consideration what features align best with your family's needs.

9.4. Evaluating Online Content

An essential step toward ensuring your child's experience with digital media is nurturing, informative, and safe involves evaluating the appropriateness of the content they consume. When assessing whether a website, game, app or an online program is suitable, consider its educational value, the presence of ads, and if it respects user privacy.

Assisting children in understanding why certain content is inappropriate helps them make smart internet decisions even when we are not around to guide them. Taking the time to check the websites or watch the YouTube videos they love together can open dialogue and provide learning opportunities.

9.5. Understanding the Privacy Policies

Many online platforms and apps have privacy policies and terms of service that define how they handle user data. Understanding these can avoid unintentionally exposing your child's personal information.

You can show your child the importance of reading and understanding these policies. Moreover, teach them the value of personal data and the risks of providing too much information online. Privacy is a critical aspect of digital safety and learning to protect it is a vital skill kids need to learn as early as possible.

9.6. Emphasizing the Importance of Balance

While managing your children's digital consumption is essential, it's equally important to help them find balance. Encourage them to engage in offline activities such as reading print books, sports, or hobbies, which can stimulate their creativity and physical development.

It's important to keep in mind that not all screen time is harmful. Quality digital content can provide educational benefits. However, it's the mindless scrolling, exposure to inappropriate content, and excessive screen time that can lead to potential harm.

9.7. Building a Digital Environment Conducive to Learning

When carefully chosen, digital tools can complement traditional teaching methods and stimulate children's curiosity. Educational platforms and games can boost their learning and creativity. Consider using applications that promote skill development, value-based learning, and creative expression.

In summary, navigating the digital world with your child can be an enriching experience if handled with care. It's about guiding them to use the internet productively, safely and responsibly. Emphasize digital citizenship and remember, becoming a cyber-savvy parent is not about controlling every aspect of your child's online world. It's about empowering them to make informed and safe decisions when you're not there to guide them.

Chapter 10. Reporting and Resolving: Handling Unwanted Online Experience

In this age of technology, it's almost inevitable that every internet user, no matter how young or old, will encounter unwanted experiences online. It's how we deal with these encounters that makes all the difference. You can empower your child to cope with these experiences effectively through accurate reporting and resolution. Let's delve into the different aspects of handling such situations.

10.1. Recognizing Unwanted Online Experience

An undesired online experience can be characterized by a variety of circumstances including but not limited to cyberbullying, receiving inappropriate content, and identity theft. Let's examine each of these scenarios more closely.

Cyberbullying could involve malicious messages, embarrassing or false information about your child posted online, or even the creation of fake profiles in their name. Receiving inappropriate content could be explicit media or violent material that's unsuitable for your child. Identity theft could mean someone else using your child's personal information and pretending to be them.

Recognizing these unwanted situations is the first major step towards reporting and resolving them.

10.2. Teaching Digital Literacy and Online Etiquette

It's crucial to talk to your child about the importance of practicing good online etiquette, also known as netiquette. Teach them about the impact of their online behavior not just on themselves but on others as well. Foster digital morals and values, talk to them about data privacy, and the importance of asking for permission before posting or sharing someone else's information or photos.

Equally important is digital literacy. It's essential that children understand the actuality of the internet world. Encourage critical thinking about any information they receive online.

10.3. Encouraging Open Communication

One of the most effective defense mechanisms is open discussion about the online experiences and encounters. Encourage your child to approach you if they stumble upon anything disturbing or discomforting online. Building this trust and communication bridge will give them the confidence to reach out to you at the time of need.

10.4. Responding To Unwanted Online Experiences

On encountering any inappropriate content:

1. Don't overreact or blame the child - understand that they're likely a victim.

2. Document the experience - take screenshots or record necessary details to provide as evidence if needed.

3. Report to the concerned body - be it the school, website administrators, or sometimes, law enforcement.

Cyberbullying follows a similar pattern, but requires a bit more caution. If your child is being bullied:

1. Let them know it's not their fault. Offer empathy and support.

2. Don't engage with the bully. Sometimes, bullies are looking for reactions, and it's best not to provide that.

3. Document and report the bullying in a similar fashion as the inappropriate content.

10.5. Using Appropriate Tools and Settings

Almost every social media platform offers users the ability to block, report and set up various restrictions. Understanding these tools and educating your child about their usage helps in maintaining a controlled online environment.

Remember to review app guidelines, set up strong passwords and encourage your child to routinely update their privacy settings on their social media accounts.

10.6. The Importance Of Reporting

Reporting these unwanted experiences is crucial in controlling and limiting such occurrences. Reporting not only shields your child from further instances but also safeguards other potential victims.

Teach your child to look out for and utilize the 'report' buttons common on most platforms.

10.7. Turning Unwanted Experiences into Learning Opportunities

While it's upsetting to deal with unwanted online experiences, they present an opportunity for you and your child to learn and foster resilience. Use these events to discuss broader life skills such as empathy, problem-solving, and handling negative emotions.

10.8. The Role of Parents in Conflict Resolution

Parents have a major role in helping their child handle conflicts and uncomfortable experiences online. It's vital to be a source of support and reassurance. Be proactive in offering advice and solutions but also let your children take the lead in resolving the issue when appropriate, to help them build problem-solving skills.

Lastly, remember that your aim is not to shield your child from the online world, but rather to arm them with the skills and strategies they need to navigate it safely and confidently.

Chapter 11. Building a Cyber-Resilient Generation: An Action Plan for Parents

The birth of the digital age has brought about opportunities and challenges unprecedented in human history. As parents, we have the responsibility to guide our children through this exciting but often bewildering landscape.

When we talk about cyber-resilience, we do not just refer to technological resilience, i.e., having secure systems and firewalls to protect against cyber threats. It also includes psychological resilience, which is about addressing the emotional and cognitive aspects of digital resilience. Together, these components synthetize into a comprehensive action plan, enabling us to raise a cyber-resilient generation.

11.1. The Essentials of Cyber-Resilience

Learning any new skill starts with understanding the basics. In the context of cyber-resilience, the essential knowledge falls into three categories: Technology, psychology, and law.

- Technology-related resilience involves understanding what threats exist - from malware to phishing schemes - and how to mitigate them..

- Psychological resilience includes understanding the emotional challenges that can arise online, from cyber-bullying to digital addiction, and effectively handling these situations.

- Legal knowledge is necessary for understanding the rights and protections you and your children have online.

11.2. Teaching Technology-Related Resilience

Keeping in mind that the Internet can be likened to a digital city with its advantages and pitfalls, teaching children about navigating this city is vital.

- **Privacy**: Teach children the importance of keeping personal information safe. Explain the risks of sharing personal details, images, or location and the measures to take to safeguard their information.

- **Security**: Go through the basics of secure practices online, including password hygiene, the dangers of unsecured WiFi networks, recognizing malicious emails, URLs, and downloading practices.

- **Digital Citizenship**: Teach them about maintaining respect and kindness online, just as they would offline. Discuss the effects and penalties for cyberbullying and the benefits of positive online communities.

11.3. Building Psychological Resilience

In a world where online interactions play a significant role, understanding emotional cyber-resilience becomes vital.

- **Managing Digital Stress**: Encourage children to take regular digital detox breaks and reinforce that it's okay to disconnect sometimes.

- **Handling Cyberbullying**: Building emotional resilience involves imparting skills to handle bullying and disrespect in the virtual space. Teach children to report and block disrespectful users and offensive content.

- **Encouraging Positive Use**: Rather than demonizing technology and the Internet, encourage positive uses, such as learning new skills, communicating with family and friends, and exploring creative pursuits.

11.4. Understanding and Implementing Legal Protections

Equip your children with the knowledge of their online rights.

- **Knowledge of Consent**: Ensure they understand the rights they have over their data, including the concept of informed consent for data collection.

- **Age Limits**: Make sure your children are aware of the minimum age requirements for various social media platforms.

- **Rights over their Content**: Teach them that they have rights over the things they create and share online, such as pictures, blog posts, and videos.

11.5. Implementing Changes at Home

Action always starts at home. Here are some practical ways you can start fostering cyber-resilience in your household.

- **Open Communication**: Encourage your children to share their digital experiences with you, the good and the bad, so you can guide them.

- **Setting Boundaries**: Set boundaries for screen time, and ensure that your children have a healthy balance of online and offline activities.

- **Lead by Example**: Kids learn from what they observe. Model yourself the behaviors you'd like them to adopt in their own digital lives.

11.6. Taking it to School

Schools play a crucial role in building a child's resilience.

- **Collaborating with School**: Discuss your efforts with teachers and school administrators. Understand their policies and work together to strengthen the safety net around your child.

- **Engaging in School Programs**: Participate in school programs that are centered around building digital awareness and cyber-resilience.

Although this action plan isn't exhaustive, it is a comprehensive starting point. Knowledge, open discussions, proactive actions, and shared responsibility will not only make the cyber world safer for our kids but will also empower them to make the most out of the digital opportunities that lie before them. In the end, our objective is not to insulate our children from the digital world, but to equip them with the skills, comprehension, and resilience to navigate it confidently and responsibly.

It's critical to remember that this isn't a task to be done once and left - it's an ongoing process, reflecting the continuously evolving digital landscape. Building cyber-resilience is a journey, not a destination. Let's make sure we guide our children on this journey in the best possible way.

www.ingramcontent.com/pod-product-compliance
Lightning Source LLC
Chambersburg PA
CBHW071042260726
48661CB00007B/3120